SERMON OUTLINES

on

The Life
of Christ

Also by Al Bryant

SERMON OUTLINES

on

The Life of Christ

compiled by

Al Bryant

kregel
PUBLICATIONS

Grand Rapids, MI 49501

Sermon Outlines on the Life of Christ
compiled by Al Bryant

© 1993 by Kregel Publications, a division of Kregel, Inc.,
P.O. Box 2607, Grand Rapids, MI 49501.

For more information about Kregel Publications, visit our
web site at: www.kregel.com

Library of Congress Cataloging-in-Publication
Sermon outlines on the life of Christ / compiled by Al
Bryant.
       p.   cm.
1. Jesus Christ—Outlines, syllabi, etc. I. Bryant, Al.
BT306.3.S47   1993   251'.02—dc20   92-26143

ISBN 0-8254-2061-x

3 4 5 6 7 printing / year 04 03 02 01 00

Printed in the United States of America

CONTENTS

FOREWORD

Beginning with the Birth of Christ and moving on through His earthly walk, these sermon outlines provide the user with a thorough and exhaustive approach to this "one solitary life." They offer a careful examination of our Savior's daily life, as it is revealed in Scripture (particularly in the four Gospels, but also drawing upon other Old Testament and New Testament texts where applicable). Varying in length and intensity, these often dramatic sermon outlines delve deeply into the meaning and message of the Greatest Life ever lived.

The compiler has also provided outlines on such diverse subjects as a comparison between the patriarch Joseph and Jesus, the temptation in the wilderness, and the impact of the Christ on such Bible characters as the woman at the well, the man in the tombs, the publican and the pharisee, etc.

It is the hope of the compiler and publisher that the use of these messages will be an effective means of challenging Christians to a closer walk and a greater understanding of God's will for their lives, and a means of reaching into the very hearts of unbelievers, shaking them loose from their preconceived notions about "religion" and its place in one's life. May these outlines help you, and may they be a source of blessing and challenge to those to whom you speak.

In using these outlines, you may want to remove the sheet (or sheets) from the book and place them in your Bible or ring binder.

AL BRYANT

TEXTUAL INDEX

THE VISIT OF THE WISE MEN TO CHRIST

"And when they were come into the house, they saw the young child, with Mary His mother," etc. (Matt. 2:11).

There were several illustrious events connected with the incarnation of Christ. One of these preceded His birth, viz., the annunciation by the angel to Mary, "Fear not, Mary, for thou hast found favor with God, and, behold, thou shalt conceive in thy womb, and bring forth a son," etc. (Luke 1:30). Then there was the appearance of the celestial choir, over the plains of Bethlehem, when they told the astonished shepherds that there was "born a Savior, Christ the Lord," etc. (Luke 2:13). And last of all, there was the visit of the eastern sages, who came from afar to yield their homage, and to present their gifts, to the newborn Prince of Life, and the Lord of Glory.

Let us notice, I. The Persons. II. The Journey, III. The Worship, and IV. The Lessons Suggested.

I. The Persons.

A. Their designation. They are styled wise men, in the original, Magi: the term is applied in Scripture to those who studied astrology and professed soothsaying and necromancy. The name is often applied to learned persons in general, and particularly to those skilled in astronomy. Very likely such were the persons in the text.

B. The country from which they came. "From the East." Some have supposed that they came from Arabia; and that they are alluded to in Psalm 72:10. But this was south of Judea. Others say, from Chaldea; but this was north. Most likely, therefore, from Persia, as this is east; and especially as astronomy had long been pursued and formed a favorite study with the Persians. Observe,

II. The Journey.

A. The cause of it. The appearance of a star; not a new planet, but some brilliant light, or fiery meteor; perhaps, that heavenly luster beheld by the shepherds (Luke 2:9). At this time, there was a general expectation that some celebrated person would appear. The Jews were expecting their long-predicted deliverer, the Messiah. The wise men viewed the meteor or star as ominous, portending some great event; and they followed its movements.

B. The journey itself. One of twelve or fourteen days; connected with great fatigue, expense, and danger.

C. Its termination. They pursued their way and persevered, until they arrived at the place where they found the young child, etc.

III. The Worship They Presented.
"They fell down," etc. In this they manifested,

A. Great faith. How unlikely to the eye of sense, that this babe was to be an illustrious prince! All appearances against it. Poor village, humble parents—nothing great—no palace, nor splendor; yet, despite this, they received Him as God's Son, the world's Messiah, and worshiped Him as such.

B. Great humility. "Fell down at His feet."

C. Great reverence. "And they worshiped Him."

D. Great generosity and self-devotion. They presented to Him "gold, and frankincense, and myrrh"—The very best! Some say, gold they offered Him as a prince; frankincense, as a Priest; and myrrh, as the Messiah, who should be cut off for the sins of the people.

IV. The Lessons Suggested as the Whole. It presents,

A. A tacit and public reproof to the Jews. They paid no regard to the event; received Him not. Even the priests at Jerusalem, who directed the wise men, moved not one step themselves. Reserved for strangers—Gentiles, to do honor to the appearance of the Savior of the world. It presents,

B. An interesting illustration of Divine Providence. The wise men's visit and the presents they brought likely provided the holy family with means to go and remain in Egypt until the death of Herod; the animals provided a dwelling and a cradle; the fish yielded Him tribute-money; and the rich gave Him a tomb at His death.

C. The true way to obtain wisdom and salvation. To observe the signs God places before us. To follow the leadings of the star of revelation, which is as a light shining in a dark place. The star of a preached gospel; for ministers are stars in the hand of Christ. The star of the Spirit's operation, "until the day dawn, and the day-star arise in your hearts" (2 Peter 1:19).

D. The homage which Jesus expects from His people. We must give Him the gold of our hearts' love and confidence; the incense of our prayers and praise; and the myrrh of our obedience.

E. Those who neglect the star of Christ must remain in darkness, unbelief, and sin.

And "he that believeth not in Christ is condemned already, and the wrath of God abideth in him."

JABEZ BURNS

"But when the fullness of time was come, God sent forth His Son, made of a woman, made under the law, to redeem them that were under the law, that we might receive the adoption of sons" (Gal. 4:4,5).

In this rich and comprehensive passage of the Word we have presented to us, An Epitome of the Scheme of Redemption—An Outline of the Gospel Plan—An Abbreviated System of Christian Divinity. Let us consider,

I. **The Important Event Stated.**
"God sent forth His Son," etc. Observe,

A. The illustrious person spoken of—God's Son. Not His creature, or servant; but His Son. Not a Son in common with believers, or with angels; but His own, His only-begotten, His well-beloved Son. "Brightness of His glory," etc. (Heb. 1:1-12; John 1:1, etc.).

B. This illustrious person was divinely commissioned. "God sent Him forth." He was appointed, and sent, and anointed for His work by God's authority—from Himself to our world—as His mediatorial Servant—to do His work, and to declare His glory. Sent by His own free and cheerful consent (John 17:4,5). Observe,

C. The nature which He assumed. "Made of a woman." The woman's seed. A descendant of Abraham. Not begotten after the course of nature; but formed by the Holy Spirit, and born of a virgin (Luke 1:30; Matt. 1:33; 2 Tim. 3:16). Hence the apostle remarks: "He took not on Him the nature of angels; but He took on Him the seed of Abraham" (Heb. 2:16). Notice,

D. The obligations to which He was liable. "Made under the law." Originally He was the divine lawgiver, and as such, was above it. But when He became the mediator, it was necessary that He should be made under it. Hence,

1. He was subject to the ceremonial law. He was circumcised—presented in the temple—He worshiped in the synagogues; went up to the feasts, etc.

2. He was under the moral law. He lived it; and in all He spoke, and did, and thought, He honored it. He kept it, in all its extent, perfectly, and was without fault; guile was not found in His mouth. He also taught it, spiritualized it, and vindicated it.

3. He was under both the ceremonial and moral law in His mediatorial capacity. He was both the victim for sin and High

Priest of our profession. He was under them, as the great sacrifice for sin, who should atone for the transgressors, bear the curse, and thus magnify the law and make it honorable (Heb. 7:26). Notice,

E.   The peculiar period of His manifestation. "In the fullness of time God sent forth His Son."

1.   The time referred to by the prophets. "The scepter," etc. (Gen. 69:10). The end of Daniel's seventy weeks (Dan. 9:24). Before the second temple was destroyed (Hag. 2:6-9).

2.   After the world had been sufficiently informed as to the event, in various ways and forms, from the first promise to the last prophecy given.

3.   When all means for man's restoration had proved totally inadequate. Various systems of religion, philosophy, and legislation, all failed.

4.   When the world was in a state of profound peace. Rome at the summit of her power. Greece in her glory.

5.   A time when there appeared to be a general expectation of Him, especially among the Jewish people.

6.   At that particular time, fixed upon as the best, by the infinite wisdom of God. Notice,

II.   The Grand Ends Contemplated in These Events.

A.   That we might obtain redemption. "Redeem those under the law." All under its authority—all guilty—all concluded in unbelief—all perishing, etc. Now, He came to redeem us from the bondage in which transgression had placed us, and from the guilt and misery to which we were subjected by the curse. Hence our redemption is from guilt, sin, misery, and eternal death.

B.   That we might receive adoption. "The adoption of sons." Be brought nigh to God; be reconciled to Him; form a part of His family; bear His likeness; possess His favor; and enjoy Him forever.

C.   That believers might thus enjoy redemption and the adoption of sons. "We" who have believed in the name of the Son of God, and thus have been privileged to become His sons. "All the children of God by faith." It is only by believing in Jesus that we become interested in the present and eternal riches of His grace (John 1:12; Rom. 5:1; 8:1, etc.) Learn,

1.   The way by which redemption has been provided.

2.   The invaluable blessings it presents before us.

3.   The importance of a personal interest in them.

4.   Exhort the guilty and perishing to believe and have life.   —JABEZ BURNS

THE LAMB OF GOD

"Behold the Lamb of God which taketh away the sin of the world"
(John 1:29).

It had long been predicted that a harbinger should be sent to prepare the way of the Lord. That harbinger was John; hence, when the people were anxious to treat him as the Messiah, he said that he was not the Christ, "But as the voice of one crying in the wilderness, Make straight the way of the Lord," etc. The very next day after this, John, seeing Jesus, said unto them, "Behold the Lamb of God," etc. Let us consider,

The Title, the Work, and the Attention which Christ demands.

I.   The Title Given to Jesus—"The Lamb of God."

A.   Jesus was distinguished for those things which the lamb is supposed to exhibit. The Lamb is the emblem,

1.   Of innocency. Now Jesus was free from all guilt and all guile. His nature was spotless; His life perfect; His conduct unblamable. He had not one sinful weakness or infirmity. The Lamb is also the emblem,

2.   Of meekness and patience. How these were displayed through His whole life. They railed at Him, despised Him, mocked Him, insulted Him; yet He endured the contradiction of sinners against Himself. This had been predicted: "He is led as a lamb to the slaughter," etc. Before the priests, before Pilate, in Herod's court, on the cross, how He exemplified the meekness and patience of the lamb. He may be likened to the Lamb,

3.   For usefulness. No creature more useful than the lamb. Its flesh is meat, and its wool raiment to us. So Jesus says, His flesh is meat indeed, and His blood is drink indeed. He also provides for us the best robe, the wedding raiment, the garment of salvation.

B.   As a Lamb, Jesus had been typified both by the paschal Lamb, and the daily sacrifices. The paschal Lamb especially had respect to Him. In its being without spot and blemish; in its being a year old; in its being taken out of the fold; in its being set apart four days; in its being slain in the midst of the assembly; in not a bone being broken; in being roasted with fire; in its blood delivering from the destroying angel. Jesus was holy—in the perfection of life. Was selected by God for the purpose. Was set apart in the promise four thousand years before His death, and entered

Jerusalem four days before He was crucified—was slain in the midst of the assembly of Israel. Not a bone of Him was broken. He endured the scorching rays of the Divine dispensation; and in His blood we have redemption from the wrath to come.

C. Jesus is the Lamb of God. His, in a peculiar sense; His only-begotten Son; His essential co-equal; His in a higher sense than angels are His creatures; His selecting; His sending; for whom He prepared a body, whom He delivered up, and whose sacrifice He accepted—His to the exclusion of every other. Notice,

II. The Work of Jesus. "Taketh away the sins of the world."

A. By His obedience and death He took away the curse of sin from the world. Whole world guilty, wretched, helpless, and condemned. Threatening of death gone forth. Jesus magnified the law in His life, and endured the curse, by being made a curse for us. By His voluntary sacrifice He bore our sins in His own body on the tree. Hence, for this He was born, and lived, and died, that He might suffer, the just for the unjust, to bring us to God. Hence it is written that "Christ gave Himself for us" (Titus 2:4). That He "redeemed us to God by His blood" (Rev. 5:9). "In whom we have redemption," etc. (Eph. 1:7). "He appeared to put away sin by the sacrifice of Himself" (Heb. 9:26). "He was manifested to take away our sins" (1 John 3:5). And He did this for the world (see 1 John 2:2, and 4:14; also 1 Tim. 2:3-6).

B. He takes away the guilt of sin by His justifying grace. Hence the Gospel which announces redemption through His blood, offers to us justification and forgiveness of sin, on condition of receiving the record given of Christ, by faith. By believing in Him we are justified freely from all things, and all our sins are blotted out (Rom. 3:24; Isa. 53).

C. He takes away the pollution of sin, by His Spirit and blood. His Spirit, by the application of His blood to our conscience, cleanses us from all sin. Hence we are sanctified by His blood, and thus wash our robes and obtain a meetness for celestial and eternal glory: "That He might sanctify the people with His own blood" (Heb. 12:24).

III. The Attention Christ Demands—"Behold," etc.

We cannot behold Him as John desired the Jews to do. He is now removed into the holiest place, etc. To sense invisible, but we may yet obey the spirit of this direction, we should Behold Jesus, the Lamb of God,

A. In the mystery of His incarnation. How low He stooped; how He humbled Himself, etc.; and how wonderful the constitution of His person. The child born, son given, Immanuel, God with us.

B. Behold Him in the wonders of His life. A holy life—a life of sorrow and self-denial, of suffering and reproach, yet of miracles, of mercy, and grace.

C. Behold Him in the overwhelming agonies of Gethsemane. Giving His soul an offering for sin. Drinking the inexplicably bitter cup. Sorrowful unto death, etc.

D. Behold Him in the sufferings and ignominy of the cross. Dragged to Calvary's summit, and there crucified between two thieves. Dying amid the darkness of the heavens, shaking of the earth, rending of rocks, etc.

E. Behold Him in His resurrection from the tomb. Once dead but alive again, and forevermore. The plague of death, the spoiler of the grave, and the resurrection and the life.

F. Behold Him on His mediatorial throne. The toil exchanged for rest; the sufferings, for glory; the cross, for His Father's right hand. John beheld Him, and said, "And I beheld, and lo, in the midst" (Rev. 5:6).

And how should we behold Him?

1. With reverence and humility. "Great is the mystery," etc. Isaiah cried, "Woe is me, for I have seen the king," etc. Angels desire to look into these things, etc. The hosts of heaven bow profoundly before Him.

2. Behold Him with shame and contrition. Our sins brought Him from heaven; tried Him; put Him to death, etc. "They shall look on Him whom they have pierced" (Zech. 12:1). The Jews who heard Peter were goaded, etc.

3. Behold Him with the eye of faith. He says, "Look unto me," etc. "As Moses lifted up," etc. "If I be lifted up," etc.

4. Behold with devout thankfulness. "Thanks be to God for His unspeakable gift."

5. Behold Him with supreme affection and delight.

Application

1. Urge all classes of sinners to behold the Lamb of God.
2. The whole world will behold Him at the last day.
3. The saints shall behold Him in glory forever.

JABEZ BURNS

THE TEMPTATION OF CHRIST

"Then was Jesus led up of the Spirit into the wilderness, to be tempted of the devil . . ." (Matt. 4:1-11).

Christ came, not only to atone for sin, but to be a perfect example to His people. It was necessary, therefore, that He should suffer temptation, that He might know how to succor the tempted. Here we have a revealed account of Christ's temptation from the prince of darkness. The whole is very minutely and fully narrated, in which we have,

I. The Time, II. The Place, VIII. The Agent, IV. The Temptation and Victory, and V. The Consolation.

Notice,

I.   The Time of Christ's Temptation.

Three very notable and important things immediately preceded it.

A.   His baptism and acknowledgment of the Father. The whole of this splendid scene is described in Matthew 3:13ff. There was the act of baptism—heavens opened—Spirit descending—the Father attested to the Savior, as His beloved Son, etc. Exultation and joy of the just often go before depression and sorrow; so with Israel, who, after joyfully leaving Egypt, were followed by Pharaoh and His hosts. So David, after His anointing, was hunted as a partridge. So Paul, after being taken to the third heavens, received a messenger of Satan to buffet him. Christ, after His illustrious baptism, was tempted of the devil in the wilderness.

B.   It was just at His entrance into public ministry. We read of no temptation during the private part of His life. But when He arises to perform the great work of His kingdom, then the devil is too active not to oppose the laying of the foundation of that empire which was to prove the ruin of His own. Those who want to be useful may expect the severest assaults of the prince of darkness.

C.   It was when He had fasted forty days. The reason for Christ's fasting is not given; doubtless, He had retired into the wilderness that He might meditate and pray before He commenced His glorious work. It is worthy of note that Moses, who was at the head of the legal, Elijah, who was at the head of the prophetical, and Jesus, who was the head of the New Testament dispensation, all fasted forty days (Ex. 24:18; 1 Kings 19:8). Observe,

II.   The Place of Christ's Temptation.

"The wilderness." Supposed by many to have been the wilderness of Sinai, a dreary, barren, and dangerous place. A striking emblem of the fallen state of the world, which He came to redeem. A just representation of what we pilgrims have to pass through on our way to the promised land. Notice,

III.   The Agent Who Tempted Christ.

"The devil." The leader of the apostate angels—the murderer of our first parents—the seducer of mankind—the prince of darkness—the god of this world—he whose nature is opposed to all that is good, and true, and holy, and whose work it is to go about seeking whom he may devour. He is distinguished for subtlety and craft, for power, for deep wickedness, Notice,

IV.   The Temptation Itself, and the Victory Obtained.

A.   To distrust the Father's care and goodness. "If thou be the Son of God, command these stones to be made bread." Christ referred to Deuteronomy 8:3, "Man does not live by bread alone, but by every word that proceeds out of the mouth of God." God can preserve in dearth and famine, when the staff of bread is broken. By His word He brings about whatever He pleases. He was then tempted.

B.   To rash presumption. Christ is conducted, most probably, to the top of Solomon's porch, which was 150 feet high, and which overhung a valley of 700 feet; and he now suggests that if Christ was the Son of God, He might cast Himself down, seeing it is written that "God shall give His angels charge concerning Him, lest at any time He dash His foot against a stone." Now, let it be observed that Satan misquoted the passage; for it is said, "to keep thee in all thy ways" (Ps. 91:11). Not out of the way of providence or duty, a most important part of the subject. Then Satan grossly perverted the passage; for the promise was not given to foster recklessness and presumption, but to encourage those who humbly trusted in the Lord, and made the Lord their fortress and refuge (Ps. 91:1,2). Christ repelled this suggestion by another quotation from the Word of Life, "It is written again, Thou shalt not tempt the Lord thy God." To rush into danger is to tempt God; and to do this, is to violate the divine prohibition. He tempted Christ,

C.   To gross and wicked idolatry. Takes Him to the most elevated part of one of the mountains in the vicinity of the desert, and shows Him, most probably, the various provinces of Judea, and offers Him these, with all their glory, if He would fall down and worship Him. Observe the terribleness of the suggestion—for the Son of God to worship the devil! The utter wickedness and vileness of it! Then the arrogant and base offer, to give these kingdoms when he had no right in them, no claim to them, and therefore, could not have the least ability to bestow any part of them. Christ draws His last arrow from the holy quiver of God's Word, and at once overcomes the foul spirit: "Get thee hence," Jesus said to Satan: "I know thy wiles and it is written, Thou shalt worship the Lord thy God, and Him only shalt thou serve"; triumphed over the adversary, for he immediately left Him. Let it be noticed how the Son of God honored the divine Word, and made it the instrument by which He quenched all the fiery darts of the devil. Notice, then,

V. The Consolation That Christ Received.

"Behold, angels came and ministered unto Him." Angels had, doubtless, witnessed the scene, and had hailed the triumph of the Son of God, and they now became ministers of comfort to Him. How relieved would be the mind of Jesus when He found Himself surrounded by those holy intelligences who had kept their first estate, the holy servants of His heavenly Father, and whoever worshiped before Him, in His holy temple! Let this encourage the saints of the Most High; they have a heavenly guard, they are in a state of happy union and friendship with angels, for they are all ministering spirits, sent forth to minister for them who shall be heirs of salvation (Heb. 1:14).

Application

Christ's temptation is intended to teach us,

1. The true character of our great High Priest, "Tempted in all points as we are."

2. The true way of overcoming the enemy, by the power of the word of truth.

3. The success which we shall assuredly obtain in the faithful use of the divine armory. And,

4. The consolation God will communicate to all His faithful and constant servants. Moreover, we learn that it is not sinful to be tempted. Satan cannot compel, only suggest; and the grace of God is sufficient for His people.

JABEZ BURNS

JESUS CLEANSING THE TEMPLE

John 2:13-25

It was perfectly right for the people to get their money exchanged, and to buy and sell sheep, oxen, and doves, but it was wrong for these things to be done in the house of the Lord. The priests were also to blame in allowing these things within the Temple.

1. **Desecration is the first thought to which I direct attention.**

The Temple was set apart for God's worship and service, therefore, to put it to a common use was to defile the house of God. Is not this an illustration of how sin has defiled man? God made man upright, like a beautiful temple, but by his inventions he has defiled the holy place of God. Our whole nature should be for the Lord. The outer court of the body with all its members, the inner court of the soul with all its affections, and the holy place of the spirit with all its capabilities. If we are self-centered, we are desecrating the sacred shrine that has already been polluted by sin. If anyone allows the idol of selfishness to be erected in his heart, he is worse than the heathen who bows down to blocks of wood and stone.

2. **Expulsion (v. 15). "He drove them all out."**

When Christ comes into the hearts and lives of those who believe in Him, He turns out all that is opposed to His will, and will keep every unholy thing out, as we allow Him to be Governor of our being, by sanctifying Him as Lord in our hearts (1 Peter 3:15, R.V.) A working man in the East End of London, in giving his experience, said, "When the Lord Jesus came into my heart, He turned out all the bad lodgers"; yes, and He will keep them out as well if we allow Him. We could not pray a better prayer than the little girl who said, "Please, Lord Jesus, come and live in my heart." Some time after she thanked the Lord for having come in, in the following words, "Lord Jesus, I thank You that You have come to live in my heart. Now, Lord, please shut the door."

3. **Question (v. 18).**

The Jews questioned Christ as to His authority for acting as He did. They were blinded by prejudice, for as Trapp remarks, "They might have seen sign enough, in His so powerfully ejecting those money-changers. The disciples call it zeal, the Jews rashness." The Jews were always asking for signs (Matt. 12:38; 16:4), and this was the one thing that kept them out of the power and blessing of the Gospel (1 Cor. 1:22).

4. Prediction (vv. 19-21).

Christ predicts His resurrection in His reply to the Jews. Godet remarks, "This answer of Jesus is sudden, like a flash of lightning. It springs from an immeasurable depth; it illuminates regions then completely unexplored by any other consciousness than His own. The words, 'Destroy this temple,' characterize the present and future conduct of the Jews in its innermost significance, and the words, 'In three days I will raise it up,' display all the grandeur of the Person and of the future work of Jesus."

5. Recollection (v. 22).

In the meantime they murmured not, much less opposed; we can do nothing against the truth, when at the worst, "but for the truth" (2 Cor. 13:8). A good memory is a blessing, if we call to mind what the Lord has done (Deut. 8:2), but it is a bane if it is the "Son, remember" to bring back to memory the evil things one has done, or the good things not done (Luke 16:25).

6. Profession (v. 23).

These believers are only make-believers. They have the King's head stamped on the coin of their profession, but the coin is made of base metal, therefore, they are counterfeits. There was a great difference in the faith of the disciples mentioned in verse 11, and the mere faith of assent to Christ's power in these, as Godet remarks, "This faith had nothing inward and moral; it resulted solely from the impression of astonishment produced upon them by these wonders. Signs may, indeed, strengthen and develop true faith, where it is already formed, by displaying to it freely the riches of its object (v. 11). They may even, sometimes, excite attention, but not produce real faith. Faith is a moral act which attaches itself to the moral being of Jesus."

7. Penetration (vv. 24,25).

The Holy Spirit seems to play upon the word "believe," as the word "commit" in verse 24, is the same as is translated "believe" in the other 99 times in John's Gospel. Christ did not commit (believe in) Himself to them, as they did not commit themselves to Him. As Luthardt says, "As they did not give themselves morally to Him, neither did He give Himself morally to them."

In chapter 2 we behold Christ discerning a man who was true in heart, and to whom Christ committed Himself (1:48), but here He does not commit Himself because He knew that these disciples were not true to Him.   —F. E. MARSH

CHRIST A DIVINE TEACHER

"We know that Thou art a teacher come from God" (John 3:2).

Christ came to sustain the threefold office of Prophet, Priest, and King. Each of these offices He fully and perfectly fulfilled. As a Prophet, He made known the will of God. As a Priest, He offered the holy and spotless sacrifice of Himself. As a King, He gave laws to His church, and remains permanently seated on His gracious throne, where He will sit until He has made His enemies His footstool. As a Prophet, He was superior to all that had ever preceded Him—greater than Moses Himself. As a Priest, He was after the order of Melchizedek. As a Sovereign, He has written upon His vesture, and upon His thigh, "King of kings, and Lord of lords." Let us at present contemplate that part of His prophetical office which more immediately relates to Him as a Teacher, and thus feel the propriety and force of the ruler's confession, "We know that Thou art a teacher come from God."

Consider then, I. Christ as a Teacher, II. As a Teacher Sent from God, III. Our Duty in Reference to Him.
Consider,

I. Christ as a Teacher.

Here two things will demand our notice: 1. The nature of His instructions; and, 2. The manner of His communications.
Observe then,

A. The nature of His instructions.

1. His instructions were diversified in their nature. He revealed the character of Deity—explained and illustrated the doctrine of Providence—exposed the depravity of the human heart—exhibited the remedy which God has provided—stated and enforced the necessity of repentance, faith, regeneration, and holiness. He published a new code of laws extending to the thoughts of men. He plainly stated the certainty of a general resurrection, and opened the glorious gates to immortality and eternal life (Matt. 5-7; John 3; 5:19-31).

2. His instructions were of great importance. The very opposite of the conceits and glosses of the Jewish Rabbi; and affording an equally striking contrast to the wild theories of the pagan philosophers. He taught man what related to his true dignity, his present, permanent happiness, and his eternal well being (Luke 4:18; John 10:10).

3. His instructions were of universal and individual concern. He was the Teacher of all classes. All stood in need of His instructions, and all were equally interested in them. He stood in the capacity of a Teacher to the whole world. His doctrines were intended to enlighten every man who comes into the world (John 1:9).

4. His instructions were of eternal consequence. The woes He pronounced on the willfully ignorant and finally impenitent were eternal, and the rewards He offered were not temporal, but eternal. For this end He came, to show men the way to everlasting life (John 10:28; 17:2,3; 1 John 5:20). Notice,

B. The manner in which He communicated His instructions.

1. With plainness and simplicity. How beautifully familiar were His discourses! How clearly He illustrated all the subjects He brought before the people! He referred them to the sower—to the fisherman—to the woman with the leaven, and the three measures of meal—to the lost sheep—to the lilies—to the vine—to the houses built upon the sand and upon the rock; and the consequence was, the common people, the plain and unlearned, who formed the great majority of His congregations, heard Him gladly. His discourses suited their capacities, and thus they received instruction, profit, and delight (Mark 12:37).
His teaching was distinguished,

2. For condescension and patience. He stooped to the poor; He sought out the wretched, and those who were overlooked by the teachers of the day. He addressed publicans and sinners, profligates and harlots; and many of these pressed into the kingdom of God. And how patiently He taught His disciples! How He endured their dullness, and with all perseverance gave them lesson upon lesson; and never did He break the bruised reed; nor quench the smoking flax (Matt. 9:11-13).
His teaching was distinguished,

3. For tenderness and affection. How deeply He felt for the poor perishing souls He came to instruct! With what graciousness He made His words known to them! How His heart yearned over them! And when they remained incorrigible He wept over them. His teaching was distinguished,

4. For truth and fidelity. Though tender and affectionate, yet He was faithful in all things to the ministry committed to Him. He was faithful to the Jews as a people—to the Scribes, Pharisees, and Sadducees—to His own disciples. He was emphatically "the truth."

And He loved souls too well to hold any part of it back (Matt. 23).
His teaching was distinguished,

5. For unwearied constancy and perseverance. He went about from place to place in search of ignorant wandering souls; and times, places, or circumstances, had no weight with Him. He cared not whether it was morning, noon, or evening; whether the Sabbath or any other day. He cared not whether His congregations were collected in the synagogue, the marketplace, on the wayside, the mountaintop, or the seashore. It was His meat and drink to do the will of His Father; and He never wearied nor allowed Himself to be diverted from it, until "He said, It is finished; and He gave up the ghost." This leads us to observe,

II. That Christ was a Teacher Sent from God.
As a proof of which,

A. We appeal to His messenger.
What did the Baptist say? "Behold the Lamb of God," etc. "He it is who, coming after me, is preferred before me, whose shoe's latchet I am not worthy to unloose." He acted as his herald, and prepared the way for Him as one sent from God (John 1:23-27).

B. We appeal to the signs at His baptism. The opening heavens exhibited it. The father's voice proclaimed it: "This is My beloved Son, in whom I am well pleased." The Holy Spirit descended on Him, and anointed Him, as a Teacher sent from God (Matt. 3:16).

C. We appeal to His transfiguration. There Moses and Elijah surrendered all into His hands—the Father's attestation is renewed; and a solemn injunction is heard: "Hear ye Him" (Luke 9:28).

D. We appeal to His heavenly doctrines. Did not His discourses attest that both the speaker and the doctrines were from above? Who could have revealed such truths, and made such discoveries, if He had not been from God?

E. We appeal to His glorious miracles. He did what no other teacher ever had done. He healed all manner of sicknesses, expelled devils, and raised the dead; and by His own power, and in His own name: hence Nicodemus reasoned, "No man could do these miracles that Thou dost, except God be with Him."

F. We appeal to His resurrection. For surely God would not have raised an impostor from the dead; but He did raise Christ; and thus He was proved to be the true Messiah, the Son of God, with power (Rom. 1:4).

G. We appeal to the influence of His teaching. Has it not made many wise to salvation? Did it not chasten the impure, reform the profligate, dignify the debased, make happy the wretched, and inspire the lost sons of men with a joyful hope of immortality? Yes; we do know that He was a Teacher sent from God.

Let us inquire, then,

III. What Is Our Duty in Reference to Him?

To receive His heavenly instructions, that the design of His teaching may be fully answered in us. In order to do this, we must receive His teaching,

A. With deep humility, conscious of our ignorance and unworthiness.

B. With constant attention, that we may learn the lessons He communicates.

C. With affectionate application, feeling that our best interests are identified with His teachings.

D. With unabated constancy, as we shall ever stand in need of His instructions.

E. With grateful acknowledgments. For His goodness and mercy toward us, and for the benefits He has conferred upon us.

F. With a practical exemplification of His doctrines in our dispositions, tempers, and lives. "Doers of the Word." See Parable of the Sower.

Application

1. Congratulate His scholars on their privileges, enjoyments, and prospects.

2. Invite the ignorant to hear Him.

3. Warn the impenitent, that all who hear not Him shall surely die.

JABEZ BURNS

CHRIST THE BRIDEGROOM OF HIS CHURCH

"He that hath the bride is the bridegroom" (John 3:29).

The Baptist was bearing testimony to Christ when he made use of the language of the text. And similar representations are given of the Redeemer in various parts of the holy Scriptures. The parable of the Virgins evidently refers to the coming of Christ as the bridegroom. The apostle, in speaking to the church at Corinth, remarks, "I have espoused you to one husband, that I may present you as a chaste virgin to Christ" (2 Cor. 11:2). And John, in the visions of the Apocalypse, was invited by one of the seven angels to behold the bride, the Lamb's wife (Rev. 21:9). One of the most rich and striking parables of Jesus contains the same implied truth, where the gospel provision is represented as a feast, which a certain king made at the marriage of his son (Matt. 22:1, etc.). We must premise that the bride of Jesus is His church, composed of all renewed spiritual persons. That in conversion they are espoused to Christ, and that the marriage ceremony will be consummated with His perfected and glorious bride, when He shall come the second time, without a sin-offering, to the salvation of His people. Let us notice, then,

I.   How Jesus Became the Bridegroom of His Church.
       He did so, both as the gift of the Father and as the voluntary act and choice of His infinitely blessed and benevolent mind. It was His own unbounded mercy and pity to man which induced Him to present Himself as the bridegroom of His church. He so loved the church as to give Himself up for its redemption, and to purchase it by the shedding of His precious blood. In accomplishing this great act of grace it behooved Him,
       A.   To assume the nature of the intended bride. Thus He became wedded to our humanity. He became of one flesh and blood with us, in being made of a woman, and in becoming in reality a child of man, and, according to the promise, of the seed of Abraham. "And the word was made flesh," etc.
       B.   To remove all difficulties to the union. These were of a threefold kind. There was guilt, pollution, and the curse. Each prevented the union of the holy and blessed Son of God with mankind. These He effectually took out of the way. He became our substituted sacrifice. He bare our sins. Became a curse for us. And opened a fountain for sin and uncleanness. He opened a clear and honorable channel for the remission of sin, the sanctification of the

sinner, and thus His elevation to a dignity, worthy of being united to the Son of God. O how great the cost of the union to Jesus! He had to redeem His bride from misery, pollution, and death. And He did this by the voluntary sacrifice of Himself. "And thus it was written, and thus it behooved Christ to suffer," etc. Well may the ransomed church in rapturous songs exclaim, "Unto Him that loved us and washed us from our sins," etc. (Rev. 1:5). Notice,

II.   **What Sort of Bridegroom Jesus Is.**
He is one,

A.   Of peerless dignity. The Son of the most high God. The Lord of life and glory. The prince of the kings of the earth. The eternal Word, of light and being (John 1:1-14). The prince of the kings of the earth. The joy of the angels, and the Lord of all. God's equal fellow and eternal delight. The governor of the universe, and proprietor of all things. Words utterly fail to describe His dignity or to reveal His glory.

B.   Of matchless beauty. All that is fair, and bright, and beautiful, is employed to show forth His loveliness. "Fairer than the children of men." "The desire of all nations." "Who is the brightness of the Father's glory, and the express image of His person." He is likened to the "rose of Sharon," and to the "bright and morning star."

C.   Of boundless riches. He is heir of all things. "The Father loveth the Son, and hath given all things into His hands." The treasures of nature, of grace, and glory, are all His. His riches are spread through immensity; they are infinite, exhaustless, and eternal.

D.   Of perfect goodness. Every excellency is concentrated in Him. His love passes understanding. His tenderness is inexpressible. His compassion fails not, and His mercy and loving-kindness endure forever and ever.

E.   Of inviolable faithfulness. Truth is the girdle of His reins. He is faithful and true. All His excellencies are, like His divine nature, immutable—"the same yesterday," etc. His mind alters not. His heart knows no change.

> His love is as great as His power ,
> And neither knows measure nor end.

Such is the character of Christ as the bridegroom of His church. We observe that He also does for His people what no other bridegroom can do. He removes all her diseases, purifies her from all her impurities, transforms her into all the beauties of His own holy image, preserves from all enemies and perils, and saves unto all the glories of a blissful immortality and eternal life.

Application

1.   Let the church see its high and distinguished exaltation, and walk worthily before Him. Let His love, and truth, and fidelity, be reciprocated. How believers should love, serve, and honor Him!

2.   Let sinners listen to the gracious invitations of the Savior, and accept of His love. He invited them to be married to Him. To partake of His grace, of His divine nature, of His immeasurable riches, and of His eternal glory. To this end, he has sent His word and His ministers to beseech and entreat them to be reconciled unto him.

3.   None but those who have Christ as their bridegroom shall enter His kingdom, or enjoy His salvation.

4.   Let backsliders return to Christ, their "first husband," for then it was better with them than now.

JABEZ BURNS

LISTENING TO CHRIST

1.   Listening to Him as our Teacher, we shall be instructed by Him (Luke 10:39).

2.   Listening to Him as our Captain, we shall have victory through Him (1 Tim. 6:12).

3.   Listening to Him as our Guide, we shall be led safely by Him (Matt. 28:19,20).

4.   Listening to Him as our Lover, we shall be jealous for Him (John 14:15).

5.   Listening to Him as our Lord, we shall render service to Him (John 13:13-15).

6.   Listening to Him as our Helper, we shall be upheld by Him (Isa. 41:10).

7.   Listening to Him as our Shepherd, we shall follow Him (John 10:27).

F. E. MARSH

"And seeing the multitudes, He went up into a mountain, and when He was set, His disciples came unto Him, and He opened His mouth and taught them" (Matt. 5:1,2).

One great end of Christ's coming into our world was to illuminate it with the light of life, and to show unto men the way of salvation. As such, His appearing had been predicted. Moses had said, 1400 years before, "the Lord thy God will raise unto thee a prophet from the midst of thee, of thy brethren like unto me, unto Him shall ye hearken." Thus, too, the apostle prefaces his epistle to the Hebrew believers, "God who at sundry times and in divers manners spake," etc. (Heb. 1:1,2). Let us then consider,

I. The Character of Jesus as a Teacher.

Now as a teacher He has been properly styled the great Teacher. Greater than the prophets. Greater and higher than the angels.

A. He possessed infinite knowledge and wisdom. The knowledge of all created beings must be limited. His was unbounded. He knew all things. As the Creator of worlds, the universe was all as transparent light before Him. He knew all the mind of God. He knew all concerning the heavenly world. He knew all concerning man—concerning death. As such He is styled "God only wise." In Him was hidden all the treasures of knowledge and wisdom. The wisest of prophets only had knowledge revealed unto them in small portions, but He had the fountain within Himself.

B. He was possessed of infinite holiness and truth. Not only was He so in essence, but in spirit, conversation, and practice. Moses was a good man, but by anger he disgraced his office, and excluded himself from the promised land. So Elijah and the whole of the prophets were fallible, erring men. But He embodied His own religion. He lived and exhibited every precept. His character was blameless. He was pure and holy, undefiled and separate from sinners. He reflected the spotless purity of the Godhead.

C. He was distinguished for unbounded goodness and love. His errand, His whole work, was one of love. It was this that brought Him to seek and to save. He went about doing good. His design was to bless, to make men wise, and holy, and happy. He came to open a pathway to the heavenly world. He had nothing in His heart but pure, disinterested, and universal love. Hence when He began His work, He stated the nature of His mission. "The Spirit of the Lord is upon Me," etc. (Luke 4:18).

D. He displayed the greatest condescension and patience. He became the teacher both of the people and the rabbis. He stooped down to their residences, occupations, and capacities. He went to the seaside and taught fishermen, laborers in the field, beggars on the highway. A poor Samaritan woman at the well. His discourses were always suited to the people—plain, simple, etc. He did not upbraid. He did not exhibit any pomp. He did not break the bruised reed, etc.

E. He enforced and ratified all by divine power and authority. He taught in His own name. He spoke as one having authority. He said, "I say unto you." He assumed the supremacy, and enforced all by unparalleled signs and miracles. Prodigies and wonders attended His steps. He healed the sick, cured lepers, restored the paralytic, expelled devils, awed the elements, and raised the dead. The people often were overwhelmed, and exclaimed, "What manner of man is this?" His promises, too, were more splendid, and His threatenings more terrible, than those of any other teacher. He opened heaven to His disciples, and showed the gates of hell to obstinate unbelievers. Consider,

II. The Subjects of His Instructions.

A. His instructions were all-important. Nothing trifling, nothing of a secondary kind. He taught great truths, relating to the soul and to eternity. His subjects were chiefly heavenly and eternal. He left nature, science, politics, and commerce to others. He revealed the glories of the heavenly world, and showed how we might make them our own forever.

B. His instructions were chiefly practical. He stated some few points of doctrine, but how seldom were those introduced. His truths were not ceremonial but practical. He told men how to live. How to act toward His Father, toward Himself, and toward each other. He spoke of the spirit we possess, the tempers we should cherish, the conversation we should cultivate, and the actions we should practice.

C. His subjects were perfect and abiding. He introduced no temporary customs. No mutable ordinances. No local institutions. He was to be the last, and therefore the perfection, of all that teachers had revealed from God. His truths were to abide forever. So His morals—so His worship—so His ordinances: baptism, Lord's supper, etc. Nothing deficient—nothing misplaced—nothing redundant in all He taught. He introduced the perfect day, and nothing shall be brighter but the light of heaven. Consider,

III.   The Claims of Christ as a Teacher.

A.   Profound reverence. This a prophet would deserve, an angel more. How much more then God's Son—His equal—His fellow; especially when we remember He is the appointed judge of quick and dead? His voice will decide the destiny of every creature.

B.   Peculiar and intense attention. Our every interest is at stake; our peace—comfort—life—salvation. If we neglect Him it will be our everlasting loss. On His lips hang life—death—heaven—and hell.

C.   The highest gratitude. His love, His kindness, His mercy—all claim this. Our interests He ever consulted, not His own; for us He said and suffered all things.

D.   Prompt obedience. This is the end of all. To obey Him—always—in all things—from the heart—with the whole life. To know, in order to do His will.

JABEZ BURNS

LOVE OF JESUS

1. The Definiteness of Love. "Jesus loved Martha and her sister and Lazarus" (John 11:5).

2. Perpetuity of Love. "Having loved His own which were in the world, He loved them unto the end" (John 13:1).

3. Favor of Love. "Leaning on Jesus' bosom one of His disciples, whom Jesus loved" (John 13:23).

4. Example of Love. "Love one another, as I have loved you" (John 13:34).

5. Record of Love. "That disciple whom Jesus loved saith unto Peter, It is the Lord" (John 21:7).

6. Attractiveness of Love. "Peter seeth the disciple whom Jesus loved" (John 21:20).

7. Commission of Love. "Jesus saw the disciple whom He loved" (John 19:26).

F. E. MARSH

JESUS AT NAZARETH

"And He came to Nazareth, where He had been brought up: and, as His custom was, He went into the synagogue on the Sabbath day, and stood up to read" (Luke 4:16, etc.)

How delightfully interesting is the history of the Redeemer! Every portion of it is full of instruction, and every incident deserves a place in the memory of the true believer. Several important events are crowded into this chapter. There is Christ leaving Jordan after His baptism, full of the Holy Spirit. Then His fasting and temptation in the wilderness: and after this, His visit to Galilee, and His wonderful teaching (see v. 15). Then the narrative of His appearance in Nazareth, etc. Observe,

I.   The Place Specified in the Text.

It was Nazareth, where Christ had been brought up. Nazareth was a small town in Galilee, about seventy miles from Jerusalem, a place of no worldly greatness nor celebrity. Here the Virgin-mother resided when the angel addressed her, "Hail," etc. Observe, too, at Nazareth "He had been brought up." Thence Joseph returned after His flight into Egypt (Matt. 2:23). When Christ was twelve years of age, and had been disputing with the doctors, it is said, He came to Nazareth, and was subject to Joseph and Mary there (Luke 2:51). It is obvious Christ still lived there, up to the time of His baptism, when He came from Galilee to Jordan. Observe,

A.   The obscurity of Christ's private life. An unknown resident in the small town of Nazareth. The Son of God, not in the metropolis; not among the rabbis, etc. Not in a palace; but in a poor family, an assistant to His father as a carpenter, until He was about thirty years old. How true that He humbled Himself, took the form of a servant, made Himself of no reputation, etc.

B.   We see in it God's estimation of the world's pomp and glory. Here was indeed a practical lesson of the emptiness and worthlessness of the world's riches and grandeur. Christ was not of this world. He came to save men from the love of its vanities, and wiles, and pleasures.

C.   We see honest industry honored by the Savior. Jesus did not exclude Himself from the useful avocations of life. He who had all majesty labored with His hands, and thus stamped industry with the greatest possible dignity and importance. Let us not forget that it was at Nazareth that Jesus grew in stature, and wisdom, and in favor with God and man. Christ had been absent for a short period, to be invested into His glorious offices and work, and now He returns to Nazareth. Notice,

II. What Jesus Did on His Visit to Nazareth.

"And as His custom was," etc. Now, here we have,

A. The place to which He resorted—"The Synagogue." These were edifices built for public worship in various parts of Judea, where prayer was presented, and the law of God read to the people. Here, public worship was honored, and stands recommended by the example of Jesus. Many would have been occupied with friends; but the honor and glory of God were ever first and last with Christ. If the heart be right, the sanctuary will have unrivaled charms and irresistible attractions. "How amiable," etc.

B. This place was identified with former associations. "And as His custom was." He had frequented it before. Yea, more, it is clear He had been a regular worshiper. As such, it would have many things to interest the pious feelings of the Son of God. Here, doubtless, He had often heard that law which He came to magnify—those prophecies, which He came to fulfill—those promises, of which He was the chief, and the sum. Doubtless, He had often longed here for the period when His mission of mercy should be made known to the people. Well, now qualified and overflowing with love, He came to the place, and as His "custom was." Holy custom! useful custom! happy custom! Many of you can feel, and appreciate, too, the truth of these exclamations.

C. The time when Christ went into the synagogue was the Sabbath. The day on which the Lord rested, and the day given as such to our first parents. Enjoined by Moses, and enforced by the prophets. It is impossible to value the Sabbath too highly. How true that declaration, "the Sabbath was made for man"; that is, for His benefit; for the cleanliness, and rest and comfort of the body; for the improvement of the mind; for the sanctification of the heart; for giving peculiarly favorable seasons for prayer, reading, worship, meditation, and preparing for a sabbatical immortality. Well has it been called the Queen of days. The Christian's Sunday; day of heavenly traffic, and holy merchandise. The type, and the earnest of that rest, which remains for the people of God. Notice,

D. What Jesus did in the synagogue. "And He stood up to read." In the Jewish synagogue they had seven readers, a priest, a

Levite, and five of the congregation. The reader always stood up; so particular were they, that he was not allowed to lean upon anything during the time of reading. Now, Jesus, therefore, honored this institution of reading the Holy Scriptures—an exercise that ever was, and ever will be, important—cannot be too much valued, and too seriously observed; an ornament to good sermons, and a corrective to bad ones. The touchstone of all preaching. "To the law, and to the testimony." Not a good sign if the reading of the Word is not greatly relished. What a majestic, heavenly sight, to see Jesus thus standing up to read the oracles of eternal truth! Observe, then,

E. The portion of the Sacred Scriptures which He read. There was given to Him the roll of Isaiah's prophecy, the part, no doubt, appointed for the day. He, therefore, unrolled it, till He came to the sixty-first chapter, and then He began to read. Isaiah has been truly called the evangelical prophet. He is so full of Christ, so clear, so rich. Christ honors Isaiah, by taking His first text from his prophecy. How wonderful the contrast between Moses giving the law, and the Messiah first preaching at Nazareth—place, spectators, subject! Thus,

1. Give especial heed to the Holy Scriptures. Oh, revere, and love, and consult that blessed Book. Be wise, and mighty in the Scriptures.

2. Let it be the test of all your views and doctrines, etc.

3. The rule of your life, etc.

JABEZ BURNS

"And He came to Nazareth, where He had been brought up: and as His custom was, He went into the synagogue on the Sabbath day, and stood up for to read," etc. (Luke 4:16ff).

In a former discourse we noticed the visit of Jesus to Nazareth, His attendance in the synagogue, and the prophecy which He read to the people. We now have to consider,

I.   The Account Which Jesus gave of His Own Mission; and,

II. The Effect It Produced Upon His Audience.

I.   The Account Which Jesus Gave of His Mission.
    A.   He refers to His divine qualification. "The Spirit of the Lord," etc. "Because He hath anointed," etc. The history of Christ's anointing is connected with His baptism. The priests of old were set apart to their offices by being washed in pure water, and anointed with holy oil. So Christ, by being baptized in Jordan, and by the descent of the Holy Spirit (3:21,22). The prophets of old were only enabled to deliver predictions by and of the Holy Spirit, "For they wrote and spake," etc. Kings also were consecrated with holy oil. Now Jesus came to sustain the threefold offices. He was the Prophet of prophets typified by Moses; He was the King of Zion, the Prince of the kings of the earth. But Jesus refers principally to His ministerial or prophetical office in the text, "Anointed to preach." Now observe, the Spirit was upon Him,
        1.   In unlimited plenty. He had the whole of the Spirit of God upon Him, not given by measure unto Him (see John 3:34). Others had it in different degrees, etc.
        2.   He had the Spirit always with Him. Prophets had not; hence we read of the Spirit being upon them to meet this emergency and the other. With Christ the Spirit dwelt and abode; so that all places, times, and circumstances were alike unto Him. He refers,
    B.   To the fulfillment of a striking prophecy. "This day is the Scripture fulfilled," etc. Every word of God is pure, true, and unalterable. Prophecy chiefly pointed to Him. "Of Him Moses in the law," etc. It behooved all things to be accomplished which were written in the law, and prophets, and the Psalms concerning Him. Now was realized the first of those striking predictions which related to His great mission (Isa. 61:1).

C.   He declares the character of His work.

1.   To preach the gospel to the poor. Pagan philosophers overlooked the poor. The scribes and rulers treated them with scorn and oppressed them. Proud, arrogant human nature generally neglects and despises them. The arcana of science, the schools of philosophy, the temples of fame, were closed against them. Jesus came to have compassion upon the multitude—the neglected, the despised multitude. He came to visit, and to pity, and to instruct, and to offer the glad tidings of the gospel to the poor. The poor especially need it; it suits their condition; and it is the glory of our Christianity, that "the poor have the gospel preached unto them."

2.   To heal the broken-hearted. Ours is a world of misery, a valley of tears; trouble is the lot of humanity. Well, Christ comes to calm the storms etc.; to bless the sons and daughters of sorrow, but especially those who are distressed on account of sin, and want inward peace. Jesus heals the broken heart. "He gives to those who mourn in Zion," etc.; He said, "Blessed are they that mourn," etc.

3.   Deliverance to the captives. Men are enslaved; the vassals of Satan; bound in the chains of vice; under the despotical sway of the prince of darkness; led captive by him at his will. Jesus came to free the souls of men from the yoke, and to give them liberty. "If the Son make you free, ye are free indeed," etc.

4.   Recovering of sight to the blind. Now here the figure is carried out. It was customary for the mind to be depressed when in a state of captivity; still more wretched by being bound in fetters; and worst of all when, like Samson or Zedekiah, deprived of sight. Thus Satan's captives are in blindness; the god of this world has blinded them; they are in darkness and in the shadow of death. Now Jesus does what no earthly power could effect. He restores the sight of the captives of Satan; He anoints them with eye-salve, and they see; He translates them out of darkness, etc.

5.   He sets at liberty those who are bruised. Who have been wounded by the adversary; or who, for want of air and freedom, are diseased: He frees their fettered feet, breaks their bands, and fills them with joy.

6.   He proclaimed the year of jubilee to the people. The very reverse of their former state; made known the joyful sound of peace and plenty, of rest and festivity. The gospel era is emphatically "the acceptable year of the Lord."

II. The Effect It Produced upon His Audience.

A. They listened with marked attention (v. 20). This was proper, necessary, pleasing. Some have their eyes closed in sleep, some gaze about, some look into their Bibles and hymn-books; but they fixed their eyes upon the speaker.

B. They were filled with astonishment and wonder. No doubt at His wisdom, but equally so at the tenderness, condescension, and love with which He spoke.

C. They were spell-bound, however, by prejudice. They thought upon His parentage and were offended by Him, and said, "Is not this Joseph's son?" Jesus replies to their private reasonings, and shows how in times past two Gentiles were honored on account of their faith: the widow of Sarepta and Naaman; and so it would be with Himself and His message.

D. They attempted to murder the Son of God. Truth flashed upon their minds, but they hated it; it exasperated them, and they tried to cast the messenger of mercy headlong down the hill. "He came unto His own. . . ." Jesus passed through the midst; He was silent; He was removed from their sight; He forsook the place.

1. To you Jesus has come with the message of life.

2. You stand in need of the blessings He bestows.

3. Do not allow prejudice to make Christ a stone of stumbling and rock of offense.

4. Embrace the message and live.

5. Put on Christ and profess Him to the world.

JABEZ BURNS

"Now when He came nigh to the gate of the city, behold, there was a dead man carried out, the only son of his mother, and she was a widow," etc. (Luke 7:12-16).

How splendid the career of Jesus! How sublime His works! How unparalleled His miracles! He spoke and acted as a God! Every footstep displayed His divinity; almighty power and unbounded goodness distinguished all His acts. How applicable these observations to the narrative embodied in the text! Observe,

I.   What the Redeemer Beheld.

It was a funeral procession: always a solemn and an affecting scene; often, however, excites no surprise, and produces no emotion. But this was,

A.   A young man. The old must die. We are not surprised to see the sun go down in the evening—the grass fade in autumn—and vegetable nature expire in winter. But his sun had gone down at noonday; leaf withered in spring, etc.

B.   He was an only son. Loss of children distressing; but especially so, when there are none left to whom our affections can be transferred. Mourning for an only son is represented in Scripture as the essence of grief (Jer. 6:26).

C.   He was the only son of a widow. One who had lost her companion and bosom friend; left to travel through the dreary scenes of life alone. Her son, therefore, would be her earthly stay and comfort; her name and family would be handed down in him; he would be her protector, solace in affliction, and would gently close her eyes in death, and receive her last prayers and blessings. But behold! the aged afflicted widow lives; and the son is cut down as a flower in all its loveliness and bloom! It is observed, too, that the mother, with a large company, were following his corpse to its long home. Probably he had been well known and highly respected. Notice,

II.   What Christ Felt.

"He had compassion on her." His eye affected His heart: besides, the whole grief of her fainting heart was before Him; He knew the whole of the matter. This was,

A.   Agreeable to His nature. He is a compassionate High Priest. His heart was full of tenderness; His heart moved with pity and love.

B. Agreeable to all His works. Compassion brought Him from heaven. His addresses, His prayers, His miracles, were all full of compassion. His life, His sufferings, His death, displayed an overflowing of compassion. When He arose from the dead, and when He ascended, He manifested the greatest compassion. And now exalted at God's right hand, as the Intercessor of man, He is still distinguished for His compassion (Heb. 4:15; 5:1,2). Notice,

III.　What Christ Said.

"He said unto her, Weep not." But was it not a harsh and unreasonable demand? To weep was,

A. In accordance with the feelings of our nature? Has not God made our hearts soft? Did He design that we should be hard and insensible?

B. Have not the best of men wept? Jacob for Joseph; David for Absalom. Did not Jesus weep at the grave of Lazarus? Besides,

C. This was an extremely afflictive case. A friend; that friend a close relative: a son; an only son: and that mother a widow; and a widow, too, in Israel; whose soul's desire would be to perpetuate her name and tribe. Still He insists that she must weep not. We shall soon perceive the reason: He was about to remove the cause of sorrow, and therefore, He said unto her, "Weep not."

IV.　What the Redeemer Did.

A. He touched the bier. Arrested it in its course; bearers felt it impossible to advance; finger of God was upon it. Hence, they stood still, astonished, amazed!

B. He commanded the corpse to arise. "Young man, I say unto thee, Arise." Although dead, he heard the voice of the Son of God, and lived. His spirit heard it in Hades—the invisible state, and came back. The heart felt the dynamic power of it, and began to heave, and warm, and dilate; the blood circulated; the cheeks flushed; the limbs softened; the eyes opened; he sat up; and last of all, he began to speak.

C. He delivered him to his mother. Christ might have insisted on the consecration of himself to His service, as a disciple, evangelist, or apostle. But his mother had need of him, and therefore, He returns him back again to her arms and to her heart. Compassion commenced, and compassion gave the last finishing stroke to this splendid and divine scene.

D. The people glorified God. The glory of God was the grand object and end of Christ's undertakings.

Application

See in this young man,

1.   A striking picture of the natural state of man. Dead in trespasses and sins; passing onward to the dark gloomy regions of the second and eternal death.

2.   Learn the only means of restoration. The powerful yet gracious word of the compassionate Jesus. "No other name," etc. He only is the resurrection and the life.

3.   God is greatly glorified in the salvation of sinners. Yes: when souls are saved, all the purposes, and designs, and arrangements of redeeming love are answered; then Christ sees the travail of His soul, and receives a reward for His toils; and God rejoices over them (Isa. 62:5).

JABEZ BURNS

LOOKS OF CHRIST

1.   Look of anger and grief, because of unbelief. "Looked round about on them with anger, being grieved for the hardness of their hearts" (Mark 3:5).

2.   Look of recognition and oneness. "Looked round about on them which sat about Him" (Mark 3:34).

3.   Look of inquiry and encouragement. "He looked round about to see her that had done this thing" (Mark 5:32).

4.   Look of rebuke. "When He had turned about and looked on His disciples, He rebuked Peter" (Mark 8:33).

5.   Look of discouragement. "Jesus looked round about, and saith unto His disciples" (Mark 10:23).

6.   Look of stimulus. "Jesus, looking upon them, saith, . . . with God all things are possible" (Mark 10:27).

7.   Look of inspection. "When He had looked round about upon all things" (Mark 11:11).

8.   Look of reproach. "The Lord turned, and looked upon Peter" (Luke 22:61).

F. E. MARSH

THE WOMAN WHO WAS A SINNER

"And, behold, a woman in the city, which was a sinner, when she knew that Jesus sat at meat in the Pharisee's house, brought an alabaster box of ointment" (Luke 7:37,38).

Observe, in this very interesting narrative; I. The Person Described, II. The Course She Adopted, and, III. The Public Testimony She Received. Notice,

I.   The Person Described.
"And, behold, a woman in the city, which was a sinner."
A.   She was a sinner. And this applies to all the children of the human family. "All have sinned." In common, then, with others, she possessed a depraved nature—heart of unbelief—practically delinquent. But there can be no doubt, that she was,
B.   A notorious sinner. Distinguished as such. There are degrees of sin. It has been supposed that she was a public woman—abandoned, dissipated, and universally known as such. A sinner above most of the inhabitants where she dwelt. But it is equally evident,
C.   That she was a mourning and deeply penitent sinner. Her eyes had been opened—her heart deeply affected with her lost estate. An anxious Christ-seeking sinner. Therefore, contemplate,

II.   The Course Which She Adopted.
"When she knew that Jesus sat at meat," etc. She had heard of Jesus. Most likely, had been brought to her present state by His heavenly discourses; and knowing now where He was to be found, she hastens to meet with Him. Observe in her conduct,
A.   Strong desires after the Savior. It must have been no small cross, for such a person as herself to venture into the dwelling of a proud, imperious, self-righteous Pharisee. Notwithstanding, hearing that Christ was there, she overcame the difficulty and came into His presence. Notice,
B.   Her deep humility and lowliness of mind. Christ was reclining on a couch, as it is the custom in the East; she did not, therefore, intrude her presence so as to interrupt the Savior, but took the lowest place, and "stood at His feet. . . . Observe,
C.   Her sighs of deep contrition. "She bathed His feet with tears." Her soul appeared to be melted within her, and her tears to flow so copiously as to provide a stream sufficient to wash the pre-

cious feet of Christ! "Blessed are they that mourn," etc. "They that sow in tears shall reap in joy." Observe,

D. Her true and hearty affection to Christ. "She wiped His feet with the hair of her head, and kissed His feet." Her hair, that which is generally the pride of her sex, she employs as a towel; and with glowing ardor, she ceases not to embrace His feet. Notice,

E. Her liberality and devotedness to Christ. She brings a precious box of fragrant ointment, worth about ten pounds of our money, and pours it upon Him, and thus anointed His feet. Perhaps, this was of the best she possessed of an earthly nature, probably her all; yet it is freely and cheerfully devoted to Christ. The power of Christ's constraining love. If this person was Mary Magdalene, as is generally supposed, it was followed,

F. By a life worthy of the public profession she now made. She attended Christ in many of His journeys—was one of the noble three who stood near His cross, when His disciples had forsaken Him and fled—and was with the first at the tomb, on the illustrious morn when He arose from the dead. Let us notice, then,

III. The Public Testimony She Received.

She had honored Jesus; and He now honors her, by testifying of her.

A. He testified to her forgiveness. He said, "Thy sins are forgiven thee" (v. 48). Pharisee condemned her (v. 39). Now Jesus justifies her—pronounces her pardoned.

B. He testified to her faith as the instrumental cause. "Thy faith hath saved thee" (v. 50). Faith is the eye fixed on the crucified Savior, which brings the virtue of Christ's blood to the healing of the soul (John 3:14, etc.). Faith lays hold of the horn of salvation—runs into the refuge—trusts entirely in Christ—and accepts God's unspeakable gift.

C. He testified to the greatness of her love. See the parable and the application of it from verses 40 to 47.

D. He testified to His approval and acceptance of her.

Application: Learn—
1. The condescension of Christ.
2. The riches of His grace.
3. His power and willingness to save the chief of sinners.
4. The true way of coming to Christ.
5. The effects of true love to Him.

—JABEZ BURNS

"Then they went out to see what was done; and came to Jesus, and found the man, out of whom the devils were departed, sitting at the feet of Jesus, clothed, and in his right mind" (Luke 8:35).

Christ Jesus came into the world to accomplish a threefold object. He came to glorify His heavenly Father—to save sinners—and to destroy the works of the devil. These three are inseparably connected. It is by destroying the works of the devil that souls are saved, and God glorified. During His ministry, Christ made several attacks on the empire of Satan. He did so in the case of the child He delivered (Mark 17), Mary Magdalene, and the instance in the text.

Observe,

I.   His Miserable Condition.

II.   His Restoration.
       And,

III. The Effects Produced.

I.   His Miserable Condition.
       See from verse 27.

A.   He was possessed with devils. Under the complete influence of malignant spirits. Satan seems to have had very great and general influence about the time of Christ's appearance on earth. "But this is your hour, and the power of darkness" (Luke 22:53). Here we see an emblem of the misery of the sinner. Satan's slaves. He rules in the hearts of the children of disobedience, etc.

B.   He dwelt among the tombs. Deserted the habitations of the living, and wandered among the sepulchers of the dead. Sinner said to "sit in darkness, and shadow of death" (Luke 1:79). The unrenewed soul, far from the favor and enjoyment of the living God.

C.   He was mentally deranged. Did not act as a rational being. When he was restored, it is said, he was in his "right mind"; therefore, not so before. Sin is insanity—the essence of folly—the veriest madness—perversion of the judgment—prostitution of all the faculties of the mind (Eccl. 7:25; 9:3).

D.   He was in a state of utter wretchedness. Naked—homeless—wandering abroad in a state of pain and distraction. A true picture of the sinner (see the prodigal; also, Rev. 3:17). "Way of transgressors is hard."

E.　He was his own tormentor. "He was in the mountains, and in the tombs, crying and cutting himself with stones" (Mark 5:5). "O Israel, thou hast destroyed thyself." Sinner ruins his reputation—destroys his health—embitters his life—and murders his soul.

F.　He was dangerous to others. "Exceeding fierce" (Matt. 8:28). "One sinner destroyeth much good." It is sin and Satanic influence that fills men with anger, wrath, maliciousness, revenge, etc.; "from whence come wars and fightings," etc. (James 4:1, etc.)

G.　No man could tame him (see Mark 5:4). They had "bound him with chains and fetters," etc. (v. 29). So, the sinner is beyond recovery by any human device or power. Philosophy has tried and failed; legislators have tried and failed; civilization and education have failed. The power of the Son of God is, alone, sufficient to deliver from sin, and to save from the wrath to come. It cannot be effected by "might or power"; but by the Spirit of the Lord of Hosts. Notice,

II.　His Restoration.

Here, several things must be observed:

A.　He was found of Christ. Christ landed on the coast, and discovered him in his misery. So, Jesus has come expressly into our world to save sinners—to seek and to save that which is lost. And Christ had compassion on him. He beheld his wretchedness, and contemplated his deliverance.

B.　The instrumental means was Christ's voice. He spoke, "and said, Come out of the man, thou unclean spirit" (Mark 5:8). What a powerful word! He tried it on the deaf, and they heard; and on the dumb, and they spoke; on the blind, and they saw; on lepers, and they were cleansed; on the winds and storms, and they were calmed; on the dead, and they lived; and now, on devils, and they trembled and fled before Him! He also speaks pardon to the guilty, and peace to the distracted. Observe,

C.　The efficient means was the divine power. "The voice of the Lord is powerful" (Ps. 104:7). His word, too, is omnipotent. "He spake, and all things were made; He commanded, and they stood fast." Gospel is the power of God to salvation. Christ has power on earth to forgive sins. He is able to save to the uttermost.

D.　The perfection of his cure. He was found,

1.　Quiescent; "sitting." No longer wandering abroad—no longer driven by the foul spirits—calm and composed. Soul found of Christ, and restored by Him, finds rest, etc.

2.   Clothed. Sensible of his shame—garments obtained. So, the soul clothed with the best robe—the garment of salvation.

3.   "In his right mind." Eye, no longer wild, but beaming with intelligence—tongue, no longer raving, but speaking words of soberness—feet, ceased to wander—hands, no longer maimed himself—an entire and complete change. So, the grace of God produces a new creation, erases the image of Satan, and engraves upon the soul the image of God (Ezek. 18:31; 2 Cor. 5:17). Observe,

III.   The Effects Produced.

A.   He desired to abide with Christ. Perhaps from fear of his old adversaries. Very proper. Soul's safety is to be near Christ. Or he might desire this from gratitude and love to Christ; attachment to his benefactor and deliverer. But Christ forbade him, and commanded him to go to his own house, etc. (v. 39).

B.   He was obedient to Christ. His will was lost in Christ's. With joy and gladness he went forth and published abroad what Christ had done for him. Pardoned souls are called to show forth Christ's power and grace, and to testify what great things He has done for them.

Application

Here is a true picture,

1.   Of the misery of sinners.

2.   Of Christ's willingness and ability to save and,

3.   The duty of those who have been brought out of darkness into His marvelous light.

JABEZ BURNS

CHRIST'S JOURNEYS OF MERCY

Mark 6:56

Of Jesus, it is emphatically said that He went about doing good; the great end of His mission into our world was to banish sin and misery, and to introduce grace and holiness. Sin had converted our world into a desert, a howling wilderness; He came to make it bud and blossom as the rose. What a contrast between the first Adam and the second; the first brought a train of evils on body, soul, and estate; the latter, a train of blessings.

I.   Observe the Characters Referred to.

"The sick." Now, sickness is the result of sin, the precursor of death; but there is soul-sickness, blindness of mind, deafness of soul, moral impotency, leprosy of pollution. Soul-sickness is the worst disease by far; it weakens, deforms, and, if not healed, destroys the soul.

II.   The Favorable Circumstances in Which Sick Were Placed.

Jesus visited their cities, etc. These visits,

A.   Were designed, not accidental. Christ had a work to do; He came to work the work of His Father; He went forth purposely, etc.

B.   They were gracious. He went not to see the works of nature or the displays of art; He went to bless the wretched sons and daughters of man: He went not to inspect the records of their guilt; He went not as a destroying angel, but as the Angel of God's presence, the Messenger of mercy, to pity, to pardon, to love; good Shepherd. "The Son of man came to seek and to save," etc.

C.   His visits were impartial. Cities, villages, country, rich and poor, Pharisees and publicans; only one qualification necessary, i.e., misery.

III.   Observe the Course Adopted.

A.   They brought their sick into Christ's way. "Streets," etc.; means of grace are the ways where Christ passes.

B.   They supplicated His healing power. "Might touch," etc. What earnestness and faith!

IV.   The Results That Followed.

Connection between the sick and Christ produced a cure.

Application

What a glorious Redeemer! What provision for sin-sick souls! Let us feel for those around us, and labor to bring them to Jesus.

JABEZ BURNS

THE WOMAN OF SAMARIA

"The woman then left her waterpot, and went her way into the city, and saith to the men," etc. (John 4:28,29).

Few narratives in the gospel history have been read with greater interest, than the history of the Samaritan woman. It presents before us a series of instructive and important facts, which cannot fail to edify the devout and contemplative mind. It will only be possible just to glance at the more prominent parts of this portion of the gospel history. The first thing which meets our attention,

I.   Is the Weary Traveler.

This traveler is on foot, in homely attire, without one sign of temporal distinction or greatness about Him.

A.   Who is He? He is the long-predicted Messiah of the Jews, the Savior of the world. Yes, you behold in that traveler the Prince of the kings of the earth. But He is now on His errand of humiliation and mercy; He is now abasing Himself, and appearing as a servant, although He thought it not robbery to be equal with God.

B.   From where does He come? He had been in Judea, teaching and preaching the gospel of His kingdom. It appears that great multitudes had received His message, and had been baptized by His authority (see 3:26).

C.   Where was He going? He was going into Galilee, and His direct route was through Samaria; therefore, it is written, "He must needs," etc. (v. 4.). You will find, in His second visit to Galilee, He wrought one of His most wonderful and glorious miracles, the cure of the nobleman's son, which ended in his conversion, with that of his whole house (v. 3). Notice, we have brought before us,

II.   A Thoughtless Sinner.

Such was the Samaritan woman. Her character is stated in verse 18; but it is evident that she was ignorant of the plague of her own heart, living without God and without hope, etc., a personal stranger to godliness, very far off by wicked works; yet she was a bigot to the national religion of her country. The Samaritans had erected a rival temple on the summit of Mount Gerizim, and contended that theirs was the right temple and the right worship. Their first temple was erected by Sanballat, after the death of Nehemiah; this was destroyed about 130 years before Christ; but most probably had been rebuilt. Now between the Jews and Samaritans there existed a most deadly hatred; beyond buying and selling, all commerce was forbidden (see v. 9). It seems, then, this woman's religion (for such she professed to have) was wrong in every particular.

    A. It was national, not personal. She had no fear of God, etc.

    B. It was based on ancient custom, and not on God's Word (v. 20).

    C. It was bigoted and malevolent, and not the religion of love. Hence see how she treated Christ (v. 9). True religion is personal, scriptural, merciful. Such, then, was the woman. Notice,

III. The Happy Meeting.

All seems accidental; Christ is on His journey; it was now the sixth hour, or about noonday; He was tired, and hungry, and thirsty; He rested during the sultry part of the day; He selects a well for the place, most likely designing to dine upon bread and water; His disciples were gone for the provision, and He is alone. But lo! a woman draws near—the person we have described; and here the Savior and the sinner meet; the Physician and the sick; the Shepherd and the straying sheep. Jesus, who knew all things, had doubtless foreseen the event. How desirable that such a meeting should take place! How essential! Some of you know the time when you first met with the Savior. Observe,

IV. The Conversation of the Savior.

He asks for water, and thus elicits her natural bitterness of spirit. He then refers to her ignorance of the goodness of God to her in His great unspeakable gift, "If thou knewest," etc. Here she evidences her ignorance of spiritual things. Christ still proposes the water of life; He then reveals His knowledge of her sinful state and life (v. 17). Here He draws an indirect confession of her sins; He removes the refuge of lies to which she had fled, and teaches her the nature of acceptable worship He declares Himself to be the Messiah (v. 26).

V. The Conduct of the Woman.

    A. She evidently personally believed in the Savior.

    B. She hastened to proclaim the Redeemer to her countrymen. "Left her waterpot," etc.

    C. She was instrumental in bringing many to Jesus (v. 30-39).

Application

    1. Now Christ is with us by the preaching of the gospel.

    2. What is the nature of the religion we profess? Do we know Him, love Him, etc.?

    3. Are we laboring to bring sinners to Christ?

    4. No instrument too feeble to be useful in His cause.

JABEZ BURNS

"WHERE IS HE?"

"Then the Jews sought Him at the feast, and said, Where is He?"
(John 7:11).

No man, having once heard of Jesus, can any longer remain indifferent to Him; he *must* take some sort of interest in the Lord Jesus.

I. Consider the Ways in Which the Question Has Been Asked.

A. Hate, ferociously desiring to slay Him, and overthrow His cause. Herod was the type of this school.

B. Infidelity, sneeringly denying His existence, taunting His followers because His cause does not make progress (2 Peter 3:4).

C. Timorous fear, sadly doubting His presence, power, and prevalence. "Where is he that trod the sea?" (Job 23:8,9).

D. Penitence, humbly seeking Him that she may confess her sin, trust her Lord, and show her gratitude to Him (Job 23:3).

II. Give the Saints' Experimental Answer.

A. He is at the mercy-seat when we cry in secret.

B. He is in the Word as we search the sacred page.

C. He is in the furnace of trial, revealing Himself, sanctifying the trial, bearing us through.

D. He is near us, yea, with us, and in us.

III. Return the Question to You.

A. Is He at the bottom of your trust?

B. Is He at the root of your joys?

C. Is He on the throne of your heart?

D. Is His presence manifested in your spirit, your words, your actions?

E. Is He before you, the end of your journey, the terminus toward which you are daily hastening?

IV. Ask It of the Angels.

They with one voice reply that the Lord Jesus Christ is:

A. In the bosom of the Father.

B. In the center of glory.

C. On the throne of government.

C. H. SPURGEON

"In the last day, that great day of the feast, Jesus stood and cried, saying, If any man thirst, let him come unto Me and drink. He that believeth on Me, as the Scripture hath said; out of his belly shall flow rivers of living water" (John 7:37,38).

The Jewish dispensation was crowded with sacrifices, ordinances, and festivals; most of these had a twofold reference: a literal one, connected with the circumstances of their institution, and a typical one, referring to the Messiah, and the blessings of the gospel. One of these feasts was called the feast of tabernacles; it was to last seven days. Its designs, etc., are fully described in Leviticus 23:39, etc. It seems the Jews had added to its ceremonies; for on the last great day of the feast, they went to the pool of Siloam, and fetched water; a part of which they drank, and the rest they poured upon the altar, in remembrance of the water supplied unto them in the desert. Jesus was present at the feast, and He stood up and cried, "If any man thirst," etc. Notice—the Speaker—the Address—the Promise.

I.   The Speaker.
"Jesus stood," etc. Remember, it was at the conclusion of this address that the officers turned and exclaimed, "Never man spake," etc. Let me refer you,

A.   To the dignity of the speaker's person: "God who at sundry times," etc. Some of those persons were of distinguished celebrity; Moses, Elijah, Samuel, etc.; Christ's harbinger. But they were servants in God's house. But, last of all, God spoke to us by His own coequal and coessential Son; a greater than Moses, etc.; one of whom the Baptist truly said, that the latchet of His shoes he was not worthy to unloose.

B.   His infallibility and infinite knowledge: He knew all things; He could not err; He saw the circumstances and feelings of all His hearers; He knew what they required; His discourses were always, therefore, direct. Observe,

C.   His mode of communication. Now,

1.   It was always tender and gracious. "A bruised reed"; "Thou art fairer"; "Grace is poured"; "Grace and truth," etc.

2.   It was always plain and easy. He never dealt in the profound; never quoted one deep saying from the ancients; no metaphysics, no glossing, no pompous terms; He simplified all He touched; He led the people to the garden, the field, the sheepfold,

etc. Hence, the poor and the illiterate were instructed and delighted, and "the common people heard Him gladly."

3.   It was always faithful and earnest. He never varnished over the condition of any of His hearers. See how He searched to the bottom of the hearts of the scribes and Pharisees. And how earnest and intent He was; it was His meat and His drink. He taught, and wrought miracles all day, and then retired, and wept, and prayed all night. He was eaten up with zeal to execute the work He came to effect. He was the preacher of all times, all places, and to all classes. Notice,

II.   The Address.
"He stood," etc. Now this address is,

A.   To the thirsty. Appetites of the body are used to set forth the desires of the soul. We read of hungering and thirsting after righteousness. Thirst is an extremely painful, and even fatal sensation, if not removed. This clearly exhibits the state of sinners. They are in a needy, wretched condition; sin, like a fever, is burning up the soul; there is no comfort, nor peace, etc.; as such, like the thirsty, they desire relief. Hence, they go up and down, saying, "who will show us any good?" Now, this wilderness world yields no pure, refreshing stream, its waters are all noxious and foul. Notice,

B.   Jesus announces to the thirsty—water. "Let him come unto Me and drink." Now, by this water we understand the gracious influences of His Holy Spirit.

1.   These, like water, assuage thirst; these satisfy the soul; pain, and anxiety, and dread are removed. Now the soul exclaims, "I have found the Messiah," "I have found Him of whom Moses," etc.

2.   It revives, refreshes, and strengthens. The poor fainting, dying soul drinks and lives, become strong and joyful in Christ, the author of His salvation.

3.   Like water, the grace and influences of the Spirit cleanse and purify; remove pollution. "I will sprinkle clean water. . . ." Produces holy fruits, etc. In Christ's address,

C.   The thirsty are invited to come to Christ for this water.

1.   Christ only can bestow it. He has the Spirit; He obtained it; He bestows. Great importance in the words, "Let him come unto Me."

2.   To come to Christ is to believe in Him; to receive

Him as the Son of God and the Savior of the world; to build upon Him as such.

3. There is to be actual participation. "And drink." Apply to our souls the fullness of Christ's benefits and blessings. Come to the cross, and look up; to the fountain, and plunge into it; to the table and eat; to the foundation, and build. Observe,

III. The Promise.

A. Christ will give him the water of life. He will impart what he needs; give him pardoning grace, adopting grace, etc., sanctifying grace; in one word, salvation.

B. He will give him a full and abiding supply. This is the idea in the text, and clearly expressed (John 4:14). "Spirit shall be in him."

C. The grace imparted shall be useful and a blessing others. "Out of his midst, or heart, shall flow. . . ." Piety is influential. God blesses a man that He may be a blessing. The converted soul says, "Lord, what wouldst thou," etc. "What shall I render," etc. Then the influence of godliness flows out. He honors Christ; brings others to Christ; talks of Christ by the way.

Application

1. Many of you have proved the truth of the text. Celebrate the praises of Christ.

2. Urge sinners to come to Christ. Come now; come just as you are; come with the sinner's plea.

3. Christians, be useful. Let your piety flow out.

JABEZ BURNS

JOSEPH A TYPE OF JESUS

	JOSEPH	JESUS
The Well Beloved	Gen. 37:3	Luke 3:22
Sent to seek missing ones	Gen. 37:15-16	Luke 19:10
Sent by his father with a message of love	Gen. 37:14	John 3:16
Was a willing messenger	Gen. 37:13	Heb. 10:7
Did not cease his journey till he came to where they were	Gen. 37:16,17	Phil. 2:7,8
Found them at Dothan (the "law" or "custom")	Gen. 37:17	Gal. 3:13
Envied	Gen. 37:11	Mark 15:10
Hated because he testified against them (last clause)	Gen. 37:2	John 7:7
The more he spoke of his coming superiority, the more they hated him	Gen. 37:8	John 8:59
Conspired against, to be slain	Gen. 37:18	John 5:18
Plans laid to deceive as to his disappearance	Gen. 37:31, etc.	Matt. 28:13,14
Brethren said, "See what will become of his dreams"	Gen. 37:20	Mark 15:29
Sold by advice of one of his brethren "Judah" (Judah, Hebrew; Judas, Greek)	Gen. 37:26,27	Mark 14:10, 20
Those who sold him acknowledged they had sinned	Gen. 42:21,22	Matt. 27:4
Endured temptation untainted	Gen. 39:7-14	Heb. 4:15; Luke 4:1-13
Was falsely condemned	Gen. 39:20	Matt. 26:59,60; Luke 23:14,15
Was numbered with transgressors	Gen. 40:2,3	Isa. 53:12; Matt. 27:38

SELECTED

"They that be whole need not a physician, but they that are sick"
(Matt. 9:12).

In the application of this proverb to Himself, Jesus evidently professed to be a physician, and His whole ministerial career will establish that profession. Christ proved Himself to be a physician of the body. He cured all sorts of diseases. It mattered not how deep, how complicated, how universal, or of how long standing the maladies were, He never failed in restoring to perfect health and soundness. Many cases which were, humanly speaking, hopeless, He restored by the word of His power. His power was so extensive that even death was forced to yield at His command. One He brought to life from the bed on which she had just expired—a second as they were bearing him to the place of burial—and a third, after he had been entombed. Jesus does not now employ His miraculous influence in healing the diseases of the body, but still His ability is the same. And though we are not called to expect His supernatural interposition in curing our bodily diseases, yet all human means will fail without His blessing.

We have seen that Jesus was a celebrated physician of the body, but He was equally successful in healing the maladies of the mind. In the wonder-working days of His flesh, He healed all sorts and degrees of mental and moral diseases. He cured the lunatic boy—He cured the demoniac, who dwelt among the tombs, and brought him to sit at His feet clothed, and in his right mind. But He also proved Himself the physician of the soul.

I.   The Soul of Man Is the Subject of Disease.

Every faculty is impaired; every power disordered. The eyes of the mind are blinded, the ears stopped, and the tongue is speechless. The afflictions of the soul are hereditary—complicated—deep seated—universally prevalent—painful—and absolutely fatal. They never exhaust their strength, or cure themselves—neither are they curable by any human agency whatever. Now, of these otherwise incurable maladies,

II. Jesus Is the Efficient Physician.

A. His knowledge is infinite. He knows the cause, the progress, and the precise state of the disease of the human heart.

B. His power is almighty. There is nothing too hard for Him to effect—He can eradicate the most virulent and confirmed disorders of the soul.

C. His tenderness is inexpressible. He deeply commiserates the misery of sin-sick souls—His heart is full of tenderness toward them—He does not want an application from them, but He seeks to heal, and says, "Wilt thou be made whole?"

D. His terms are astonishing. He heals without money, and without price—all He desires is the use of His medicines, and humble attention to the prescriptions He gives.

E. His success is infallible. He never fails to effect a cure—none ever sought His aid in vain. Though death had already commenced its ruinous work upon the dying malefactor, yet one word of His healed the malady of his soul, and saved him from the jaws of eternal death, and prepared him for the healthy abodes of the heavenly paradise.

F. As a physician, Christ's invitations are universal. He does not confine His practice to any grade or class of society: the world is His hospital; and all mankind may become His patients: the poor are alike welcome with the rich: He heals all who come unto Him. Notice,

III.   The Method of Healing Which He Adopts.
In curing the diseases of the soul,

A. He employs the agency of His word. It is said He sent His word, and healed them; the word contains a revelation both of the disease and mode of cure: the word is emphatically the word of salvation—the word of life. He also employs,

B. The balm of His blood. The blood of Jesus is the true balm of Gilead—that in which alone we have redemption, even the forgiveness of sin. It is this which speaks peace to the guilty mind, and which cleanses from all unrighteousness.

C. By the power of His Spirit. The Spirit applies the precious blood of Christ to the heart, and thus the malady of sin is removed, and the soul is made whole.

Application
1.   The cure which Christ imparts to the sin-sick soul is radical, universal, and abiding. He heals every wound, and restores every faculty: He gives beauty for deformity; strength for weakness; and blooming health for sickness and decay.
2.   How important that we ascertain our true state and

condition. Has He healed us? Have we been convicted of sin—have we loathed it—and have we been delivered from it? Have we the signs of spiritual health upon us? Do we live in the exercise of godliness? Is the pain and smart, arising from consciousness of sin, removed? Have we the indwelling of the Spirit testifying that we are the sons of God?

3.   Let spiritual health be carefully cultivated. Avoid all that is pernicious to the soul. Cherish the influences of the Spirit, and thus grow in grace, and in the knowledge of the Lord Jesus Christ.

4.   The spiritually sick, who despise this physician, must inevitably perish. There is no other balm in Gilead, nor any other physician there.

JABEZ BURNS

J-E-S-U-S

When John Howard wanted to visit the prisons of Russia he sought an interview with the Czar. He explained his object, and the Czar gave him permission to visit any prison in his Empire. It was a long and weary journey; he knew how jealously the prisoners were guarded, and how averse the jailers were to permit anyone to visit them. But he set out in perfect confidence. When he arrived at a prison he would make his application, and was prepared for the refusal which invariably came. Then he produced the Czar's mandate, and the prison doors were immediately opened to him. He had faith in that name, and was justified by the results. In like manner, those who have faith in Him who bear the name of Jesus, find that there is in that name:

J --Justification ------(Rom. 4:24,25)

E --Eternal Life------(John 4:13,14).

S --Salvation----------(Matthew 1:21).

U --Union ------------(John 12:24).

S --Satisfaction-------(John 7:37).

F. E. MARSH

THE MIRACLES OF THE LOAVES AND FISHES

"And when it was evening, His disciples came to Him, saying, This is a desert place, and the time is now past; send the multitude away" *(Matt. 14:15-21).*

Christ performed such mighty works as no other man did. His miracles were numerous, public, full of mercy and compassion, and were all performed by His own power and in His own name. Let us at present consider the miracle of the loaves and fishes; and in doing so, I. Explain and Illustrate the Various Circumstances Connected with It, and notice II. The Spiritual Lessons Which It Teaches.

I.   **Explain and Illustrate the Various Circumstances Connected with the Miracle.** Notice,

A.   The occasion of the miracle. Christ had been healing and teaching the people; the multitude had been so deeply interested as to forget the necessary wants of the body; were ready to faint for want of food.

B.   The place where the miracles were wrought. It was "a desert place." Had they been in a city or village where provision could have been obtained, a miracle would have been unnecessary. Christ never wrought one superfluous miracle. Here it was necessary that He should convince the people that He could spread a table for them in the wilderness.

C.   The laudable anxiety of the disciples. They desired that the people might be dismissed, that they might retire and buy food in the villages. This was considerate and humane. We ought never to forget that our fellow-creatures have bodies as well as souls; and if we see a brother or a sister hungering and feel not for them, how dwells the love of God in us? Notice,

D.   The surprising reply of the Redeemer. "They need not go away." Not only was the Messiah in the midst of them, but that Messiah was the God of nature and providence; His hands were daily opened for the supplying of every living thing with good. He then directed them to see what provision they possessed. This was necessary, that it might appear, first, that a miracle was really indispensable; and secondly, that the miracle might appear in its true and real character. It was found that five loaves or biscuits, and two small fishes, were all the provisions they could collect. How totally inadequate to the demands of the many thousands, the hungry multitude! Observe,

E. The commands Christ gave to His disciples.

1. That the provisions should be brought to Him. He did not despise and cast away the loaves and fishes; but made them, as it were, the seed-corn of that abundant supply which He was about to provide. The loaves and fishes were quite unavailing in the hands of the disciples; therefore, Christ received them that His almighty power might be employed upon them.

2. He commanded the multitude to sit down. That all might be done in order; that the number might be accurately ascertained; and that all might be easily and fully supplied. Then notice,

F. Christ's conduct with respect to the provisions. He took it, lifted up His eyes to heaven, gave thanks, blessed it, and broke it. What an example of piety and devotion! How anxious to acknowledge and glorify His Father! What majesty and glory would be seen in the face and actions of Jesus on this occasion! Then notice,

G. The mode of distribution adopted. "He gave it to His disciples, and they gave it to the people." Thus did He exhibit His leadership and authority, and thus did He recommend His disciples to the people, as the distributors of His bounty, and the officers of His kingdom. Then observe,

H. The creation and multiplication of the food which took place. The disciples went forth, supplying each with an abundance; and as they distributed, it increased in their baskets, so that 5,000 men, besides, no doubt, as many more women and children, ate and were filled. Notice,

I. The lesson of frugality which Jesus taught. He then said: "Gather up the fragments, that nothing be lost." And behold, twelve baskets of fragments remained! Many thousand times more than the stock with which the meal was commenced! God is the source of abundance; but He will not sanction extravagance or waste. Let us consider,

II. The Spiritual Lessons Which the Miracle Affords.

A. In the people we see a striking representation of the moral condition of the human family. In a desert world—starving for want of food—no human means of supply.

B. In the provision we see a true exhibition of the blessings of the gospel. Its source, Jesus; its apparent insufficiency, yet its abundance, yea, inexhaustibleness. Its freeness and cheapness; without money and without price. Its satisfying nature; all ate and were filled.

C. In its distribution we see the nature of the office of the

Christian ministry. It is—to receive from Christ's hands the bread of life, and to give it to a dying world. It is Christ's provision only they are to distribute.

D. In the abundance remaining we see the boundlessness of gospel supplies. Myriads have eaten, and yet the bread is undiminished. We learn,

E. That personal participation of gospel blessings is necessary to our happiness and satisfaction. We must not only be of the multitude, and hear, and see, and sit down with them; but we must, also, eat, receive Christ into our hearts by faith; and thus only can we enjoy the blessings of God's great, and full, and abundant salvation. The invitation is: "Come ye, buy and eat; . . . and milk, without money, and without price."

JABEZ BURNS

THREE APPEARINGS OF CHRIST

Hebrews 9:24-28

It must be remarked that the words rendered "appear" in Hebrews 9:24-28 are three different words in Greek.

1. The past appearing (9:26).

Here the word "appear" means, for one to be seen who had been hidden, as when one comes from behind a curtain which had concealed him.

2. The present appearing (9:24).

The term here indicates appearing in an official sense. Christ now appears in the presence of God, as the Representative of His people, to plead on their behalf, and to look after their interests.

3. The future appearing (9:28).

Here it signifies to see face to face, as when Paul saw Jesus, when he was on his way to Damascus (1 Cor. 15:8).

F. E. MARSH

"Having loved His own which were in the world, He loved them unto the end" (John 13:1).

We have in the text, I. A Peculiar Description of Believers—Christ's own, II. Their Present Condition—"In the world," and III. Christ's Unalterable Attachment to Them—"Having loved them, He loved them to the end." We have,

I.   A Peculiar Description of Believers.

They are Christ's own. No doubt this referred originally to the disciples of Jesus; but it is equally applicable to all who shall believe upon Him to the end of the world. Believers are Christ's own.

A.   They are His own by purchase. "Redeemed by His blood." "Bought with a price." "He loved them, and gave Himself for them."

B.   They are His own by gift. They are given to Him by His heavenly Father. As His seed—His reward—the travail of His soul, etc. (John 6:37-40; 10:29).

C.   They are His own by a cheerful and entire consecration of themselves to His service.

Given themselves to the Lord. Left all and followed Him. Yielded themselves to His service. "This God shall be our God forever," etc.

D.   They are Christ's own, as they bear His image, and manifest His Spirit. Christ dwells in them by His Spirit, and they are changed into His image. Same mind in them that was in Christ. He is their example, and they tread in His steps.

II.   Their Present Condition.

"In the world." Not of the world. Brought out of it. Saved from it. Crucified to it. But they are in it. As strangers and pilgrims on their way to another and a better world. They are in the world,

A.   For their own sake. To be instructed, and that they may grow in grace, in knowledge, and in holiness, and be thus made meet for the celestial inheritance. Here they have to labor, wrestle, and run the race set before them.

B.   For Christ's sake. To profess Him. To testify of Him. To be His witnesses. His living epistles. His avowed friends.

C.   For the world's sake. They are the pillars of the world.

The lights of the world. The salt of the earth. They are blessings to it, by their example, by their counsels, and by their prayers. Sodom would have remained to this day had ten righteous persons been found in it. Jerusalem was not destroyed until Christ's disciples fled out of it. Notice,

III.   Christ's Unalterable Attachment to Them.
       "Having loved them, He loved them to the end."
       A.   Christ loved them when He freely gave Himself a ransom for their souls. "Herein is love," etc. "Greater love hath no man," etc. "Unto Him who loved us," etc.
       B.   Christ loves them as His believing disciples. He loves them with complacency and delight. His heart is set upon them. His words—His smiles—His communications to them, are all evidences of His love. They are His flock, His jewels, etc. (John 15:9). He pities them. Bears with them. Keeps them. Blesses them. Saves them, etc.
       C.   Christ loves them unchangeably. "Unto the end." In life—health—sickness—death—and forever and ever. His love is ardent—abiding—increasing—inconceivable, and everlasting (Eph. 3:19; Jer. 31:3).
       How distinguished the character, how responsible the station, and how happy the privilege of the people of God!

JABEZ BURNS

SIX FACTS ABOUT THE PUBLICAN IN RELATION TO CHRIST

1.   He knew what he was, the sinner (Luke 18:13, R.V.).

2.   He knew where he was, at a distance (Luke 18:13).

3.   He knew how he felt, ashamed (Luke 18:13).

4.   He knew what he needed, mercy or propitiation (Luke 18:13).

5.   He knew where to get it, God (Luke 18:13).

6.   He knew he had it, went to his house justified (Luke 18:14).

CHARLES INGLIS

"Sir, we would see Jesus" (John 12:21).

The text was the language of certain Gentile proselytes, who had come up to worship at the feast of Jerusalem; and who came to Philip, and said, "Sir, we would see Jesus." Let us consider,

I.   **What This Desire Implies.**
It implies,
A.   Some knowledge of Christ already. They had heard of Him, His name was familiar to them. They had some idea of His pretensions to the Messiahship, etc. It implied,
B.   An ardent longing that this knowledge might be increased. What they knew was insufficient for experimental and practical purposes. Might be very limited, and in many things erroneous. Correct view of Christ of the greatest importance. We should know Him in His titles—in His offices—and in His work. We should know Him personally—savingly, etc. It included,
C.   The employment of proper means to increase this knowledge. They came to Philip, inquired, etc. So we are called upon to "hearken to Jesus," to "come to Him," to "behold Him." We have His word where He is revealed—His ordinances where He is exhibited—His gospel where He is published. Notice,

II.   **The Reasons on Which This Desire May Be Grounded.**
A.   On account of what may be seen in Christ. There is to be seen in Christ what is not to be seen elsewhere. In Christ there is—
1.   The brightest display of the Divine glory. "We behold His glory, the glory of the only-begotten of the Father," etc. Glory of God exhibited in the works of nature and providence, but in Christ it is concentrated. Fullness of the Godhead dwelt in Him bodily. There is to be seen in Christ,
2.   The clearest manifestation of the Divine perfections. In Him were exhibited—boundless knowledge—almighty power—exuberant goodness—unsullied purity—and infinite mercy. In Christ is to be seen,
3.   The only mediator between God and man. The sinner's days-man, standing between the culprit and the offended Deity, with His hands upon them both. Only way to the Father. The true ladder, reaching from earth to heaven. In Christ is to be seen,
4.   The depository of all spiritual blessings. In Him "all

fullness dwells." "Full of grace and truth." Pardon for the guilty—peace for the unhappy—purity for the defiled—salvation for the lost, and eternal life for all who believe. This desire to see Christ may be grounded,

B. On the advantages arising from a believing sight of Him. A believing sight of Jesus,

    1. Enlightens the mind. "He is the true light, and believers become the children of light, walking in the light," etc. It,

    2. Cheers and comforts the heart. "Then were the disciples glad when they saw the Lord." See instances, Andrew, Simon, Philip, etc. (John 1:40); woman of Samaria (John 4:28). It,

    3. Transforms the soul. "But we all with open face, beholding as in a glass the glory of the Lord, are changed into the same image," etc. (2 Cor. 3:18). Let us,

III. Specify Some Circumstances When This Desire Is Particularly Seasonable.

A. When the soul is burdened with a sense of guilt. No other name that can charm—no other voice that can speak peace—no other who possesses healing virtue, etc. Moses not desired—prophets of no avail—apostles cannot suffice. The language of the heavy-laden heart is, "Sir, I would see Jesus."

B. In the day of trouble and affliction. He sympathizes—His presence supports—His grace is sufficient.

C. In the means of grace. What is the Word without Christ? Prayer or praise without Him? What is baptism or the supper, without Jesus there?

D. In the hour of dissolution. His rod and staff only can comfort. He guides through the valley. When friends fail us—when flesh decays and heart fails—"He is the strength of our heart, and portion forever" (Stephen; Acts 7:55). And the view of faith in the dying Christian, shall immediately be followed by the full and open vision of the Redeemer in His kingdom, where they shall be like Him, for they shall see Him as He is.

Application

    1. Invite the sinner to "behold the Lamb of God."

    2. Urge him to look unto Him and be saved.

    3. Let the believers look unto Jesus, "the author and finisher of our faith," etc. Make Him the model of their obedience, and the object of their supreme adoration and love.

JABEZ BURNS

CHRIST THE WAY TO HEAVEN

"I am the way" (John 14:6).

The Christian is professedly a pilgrim, a pilgrim on his way to glory. He is seeking a better country, that is to say, a heavenly one. He looks upward beyond the glittering starry skies. To this world of happiness and rest, Jesus is the way,

I.   By the Revelation He Gave of It.

A clear description of that blessed world was never given until Jesus was manifested in the flesh, and brought life and immortality to light by His gospel. He spoke of it in the most plain and familiar terms, called it His "Father's house," the place of many mansions. And on some occasions He referred to its purity, and its celestial glory. How splendid must the imperial palace of Jehovah be!—the seat of His heavenly court, the residence of His spiritual and glorious hosts, where He is seated on His high and lofty throne, in overwhelming splendor of eternal light. To dwell in the presence of God is supreme joy and eternal life. Here are pleasures forevermore.

II.   Christ Is the Way Also, Because He Only Can Confer the Title to the Possession of Heaven.

Heaven is the inheritance, and we become heirs through the justifying grace of Jesus. By faith in His mediatorial work, we become the sons of God, and joint heirs with Jesus Christ.

III.   Jesus Also Imparts the Preparedness Necessary to Its Enjoyment.

Before it can be enjoyed, we must be prepared; this He effects by the cleansing power of His blood, as communicated by the sanctifying influences of the Holy Spirit. Thus He makes us partakers of His own nature, and renders us capable of participating in His glory.

IV.   Then He Is the Way, as He Is Our Glorious Leader and Example.

He is the guide of His people, and He left us an example, that we should follow His steps. He, as our forerunner, has gone before, and has opened a new and living way into the holiest place, and has consecrated it for us, by His precious blood. No man can come to the possession of the Father's favor on earth, or the possession of the glory He bestows in heaven, but through Him.

V. Jesus Is the Only Way to Eternal Glory.

There is but one mediator between God and man, the man Christ Jesus. He is the one immutable foundation, the rock of ages, and other foundation can no man lay than that is laid, which is Christ. To Him, as the way, all the prophets testified; and John, as His illustrious harbinger and herald, proclaimed Him as the Lamb of God, who takes away the sins of the world. It is the special work of the ministry, to point inquiring, penitent souls to Jesus, as the only Refuge and Savior from the wrath to come. And in doing this, the distinguishing features of this way must be specified.

A. Its freeness must be proclaimed; that it is not restricted to a select few of mankind, but that Christ is the Savior of all men, especially of those who believe. That there is no condition, natural or moral, which can exclude from Jesus and His salvation, but the self-willed and persevering exercise of unbelief. He has declared that whosoever comes to Him He will in no wise cast out.

B. Then its gratuitousness must be announced. As it is free to all, so it is free to all on the most gracious terms; there is no moral fitness required. No meritorious service is demanded. Unworthy, wretched, and truly despicable, and rebellious sinners, may approach Jesus as they are.

C. Then it is a way of sure and certain blessedness. All who have received Jesus, and walk in Him, possess peace and joy in the Holy Spirit. Their course infallibly tends to eternal life. No evil can come near them, no mischief can befall them. Abiding in Him they cannot perish, neither can any pluck them out of His hands. They go from strength to strength—everyone of them at last appears before God in His celestial Zion.

> Jesus, my Lord, thou only art
> Salvation's blessed way,
> Oh, cheer my heart, and keep my feet
> Unto eternal day.

JABEZ BURNS